The INSIDE GUIDE

FAMOUS NATIVE AMERICANS

Squanto

By Ann Byers

Cavendish Square

New York

Published in 2021 by Cavendish Square Publishing, LLC
243 5th Avenue, Suite 136, New York, NY 10016

Copyright © 2021 by Cavendish Square Publishing, LLC

First Edition

This publication represents the opinions and views of the author based on his or her personal experience, knowledge, and research. The information in this book serves as a general guide only. The author and publisher have used their best efforts in preparing this book and disclaim liability rising directly or indirectly from the use and application of this book.

All websites were available and accurate when this book was sent to press.

Library of Congress Cataloging-in-Publication Data

Names: Byers, Ann, author.
Title: Squanto / Ann Byers.
Description: First edition. | New York : Cavendish Square, Publishing, LLC,
2021. | Series: The Inside Guide: Famous Native Americans | Includes
bibliographical references and index.
Identifiers: LCCN 2019042079 (print) | LCCN 2019042080 (ebook) | ISBN
9781502650627 (library binding) | ISBN 9781502650603 (paperback) | ISBN
9781502650610 (set) | ISBN 9781502650634 (ebook)
Subjects: LCSH: Squanto—Juvenile literature. | Wampanoag
Indians—Biography—Juvenile literature. | Pilgrims (New Plymouth
Colony)—Juvenile literature.
Classification: LCC E99.W2 B94 2021 (print) | LCC E99.W2 (ebook) | DDC
974.4004/973480092 [B]—dc23
LC record available at https://lccn.loc.gov/2019042079
LC ebook record available at https://lccn.loc.gov/2019042080

Editor: Kristen Susienka
Copy Editor: Rebecca Rohan
Designer: Deanna Paternostro

The photographs in this book are used by permission and through the courtesy of: Cover Kean Collection/Archive Photos/Getty Images; pp. 4, 6, 25, 28 (top right, bottom right) © North Wind Picture Archives; p. 7 Stefano Bianchetti/Corbis via Getty Images; p. 8 Science History Images/Alamy Stock Photo; p. 10 Harold M. Lambert/Kean Collection/Archive Photos/Getty Images; p. 12 Pineese WED/Wikimedia Commons; p. 13 Jonathan Wiggs/The Boston Globe via Getty Images; p. 14 Private Collection/ Peter Newark Pictures/Bridgeman Images; pp. 14-15 Barney Burstein/Corbis/VCG via Getty Images; p. 16 Archive Photos/Getty Images; p. 17 duncan1890/DigitalVision Vectors/Getty Images; p. 18 MPI/Getty Images; pp. 19, 26 Marcio Jose Bastos Silva/ Shutterstock.com; p. 21 Michael Sean O'Leary/Shutterstock.com; p. 22 American School/Bridgeman Images; p. 24 TCD/Prod.DB/ Alamy Stock Photo; pp. 26-27 Monkey Business Images/Shutterstock.com; p. 27 (top) Stock Montage, Inc./Alamy Stock Photo; p. 28 (top left) Three Lions/Hulton Archive/Getty Images; p. 28 (bottom left) American School/Getty Images; p. 29 (left) Bettmann/Bettmann/Getty Images; p. 29 (right) Universal History Archive/Universal Images Group via Getty Images.

Some of the images in this book illustrate individuals who are models. The depictions do not imply actual situations or events.

CPSIA compliance information: Batch #CS20CSQ: For further information contact Cavendish Square Publishing LLC, New York, New York, at 1-877-980-4450.

Printed in the United States of America

Find us on

CONTENTS

Chapter One: 5
   Heroes Everywhere

Chapter Two: 11
   A Helper and Friend

Chapter Three: 17
   Different Worlds

Chapter Four: 23
   Remembering Squanto

Think About It!   28

Timeline   29

Glossary   30

Find Out More   31

Index   32

Shown here is a Wampanoag warrior. This group of Native Americans played an important part in the history of the United States.

HEROES EVERYWHERE

History has many different tales about men and women who did incredible things. These people are known as heroes. Groups of people around the world tell stories of their heroes and their bravery, intelligence, or amazing deeds. Heroes can be real or fictional, and real heroes have truly earned their place in history.

The Native American tribes living in the United States today have many legends and stories of important people. These men and women have become heroes over generations. Some people might be well known, such as Pocahontas or Sacagawea. Others might be new names, such as Sequoyah or Crazy Horse. All of their stories helped shape America into what it is today.

One of the most-told stories about Native Americans involves a man named Squanto. He was an important part of the story of Europeans arriving in America. He was also at the first celebration of what we now call Thanksgiving. In fact, he made this celebration possible. His story lives on in US history.

Fast Fact

Thanksgiving is celebrated every November in the United States. Canada celebrates Thanksgiving, too, but it honors a different feast and happens in October.

The first Native American the Pilgrims met was Samoset (*center*).

This illustration shows the first time Massasoit—a Wampanoag leader—visited the Pilgrims.

Squanto

Squanto was born in the later 1500s, during a time when American cities didn't exist. America itself was a landmass and not its own country. Squanto's surroundings were forests, rivers, and mountains. He belonged to a Native American tribe called the Patuxet. They were part of a larger group called the Wampanoag. His tribe called him Tisquantum. However, later in life, he became known as Squanto. Today, people know him by that name.

Fast Fact

A Native American chief named Samoset was the first person to make contact with the Pilgrims in 1620. He and Squanto worked together.

WHO WERE THE PILGRIMS?

The Pilgrims were a group of men and women who traveled in 1620 from England to North America. Their original destination was the colony of Virginia; however, a storm blew them off course. They landed in Plymouth Harbor in Massachusetts instead. The ship that brought them to America was called the *Mayflower*.

The Pilgrims were seeking religious freedom. That means they wanted to practice religion in a way that differed from how others practiced in England. They believed in a certain way of life and had strict rules for following Christianity.

Some people aboard the *Mayflower* weren't looking for religious freedom. The Pilgrims called these people "strangers." Anyone who was a believer was called a "saint." The strangers didn't practice the Pilgrims' strict Christianity, but they wanted a new life in America. They agreed to listen to the Pilgrims and follow new rules in the new land.

Before they left the *Mayflower*, most of the men on the ship signed an agreement called the Mayflower Compact. This was the first set of rules or laws written down for a group of settlers to follow in the New World. It would be an important example for other similar agreements in later generations.

The Pilgrims brought to the New World the few things they thought they would need to start new lives.

European settlers were just beginning to arrive in North America during Squanto's lifetime. They traded with native groups. Soon, much of the place Squanto knew would change forever.

In the 1600s, people from across the Atlantic Ocean landed near Squanto's home. They came from England, looking for a new place to live and practice their religion. That's why they're known as the Pilgrims. They called North America the New World.

Fast Fact

In total, 41 men signed the Mayflower Compact of 1620. Women weren't invited to sign.

Squanto would play a key role in relationships between these English settlers and the Native American people. His knowledge of the English language and of farming techniques made him very important to his tribe and the settlers. Without him, war might have happened, or people might have starved.

This is the story of Squanto's life and the time in which he lived. Let's learn more about him!

This painting shows the Pilgrims on the *Mayflower* arriving on land.

A HELPER AND FRIEND

In the 1500s, North America was a different place. Not many Europeans had settled there. Native Americans made up the majority of humans living in what's now the United States. They had their own homes, rules, beliefs, and legends. Sometimes they fought with other native groups. Other times, they made peace.

The 1600s brought much change to this land and the people living there. Their lives would never be the same. One person whose life changed was Squanto. He's remembered as a helpful Native American whose life is still celebrated today.

Kidnapped!

The story of Squanto is often told around Thanksgiving. No one knows for sure if the story is completely true. According to this story, Squanto was born sometime between 1575 and 1590. He was a Patuxet, a Native American from one of the many Wampanoag tribes that lived in what's now called New England.

When Squanto was a young man, explorers from England came to the area where he

Fast Fact
The Pilgrims settled in what had been the Patuxet's summer village.

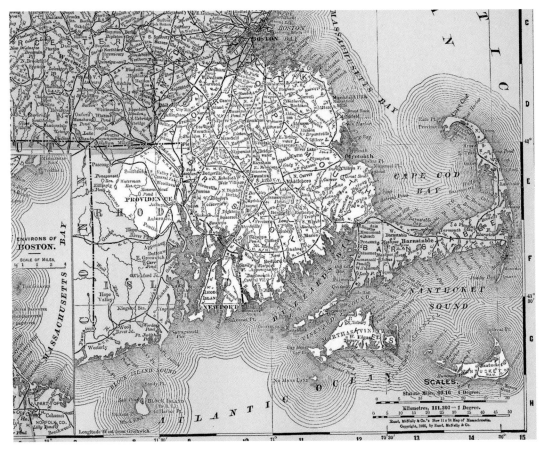

The yellow area on this map shows where the Wampanoag lived in the 1600s.

lived. When the men on the ship came ashore, they seemed friendly, but Squanto quickly learned they were not! They kidnapped him and some other Patuxet. They took them to Spain and then to England. For five years, Squanto lived across the ocean from his homeland. Eventually, he came back to his home in what's now Massachusetts.

When he returned to his village, it was empty. Not one person was around. It seems likely that the strange men who captured

Fast Fact

Tisquantum meant "rage."

THE WAMPANOAG

The Wampanoag are Native Americans. In the 1600s, they lived in what are now the states of Massachusetts and Rhode Island. "Wampanoag" means "People of the First Light." They were the first people to see the sun when it rose above the ocean every day. In warm months, they lived near the coast. There they grew beans, squash, and maize, which is a kind of corn. They fished in the rivers and the ocean. In the winter, they moved to the forests, where they hunted for food.

Thousands of Wampanoag lived in more than 60 villages. Each village was for a separate tribe. They were usually friendly and peaceful. Sometimes they fought the Narragansett, a different tribe. The two groups hunted and fished near each other.

Today, 4,000 to 5,000 Wampanoag live in Massachusetts. They live just like other Americans, and they also teach their children traditional stories and ways of life.

Wampanoag today dress like other Americans, but they wear traditional clothes for special events.

Squanto had also brought diseases with them, and the diseases had killed thousands of Native Americans—including the people who lived in Squanto's village. Squanto was the only Patuxet still alive. Sad and lonely, he went to live with another Wampanoag tribe. The Wampanoag leader who allowed him to live with his tribe was named Massasoit.

The Pilgrims Arrive

Squanto's world changed again a short time later when the Pilgrims arrived in 1620. They had a large ship, wore strange clothes, and built different houses.

At first, the Wampanoag didn't trust the Pilgrims. They were English, and the Wampanoag thought the English were all kidnappers. However, the Pilgrims had powerful guns. Massasoit thought if he could make friends with the Pilgrims and possess guns, all the other tribes would be afraid of him.

Massasoit first sent Samoset to speak to the Pilgrims. Samoset was a Native American from Maine who had arrived in Massasoit's territory a few weeks earlier. He knew a few words of English and amazed the Pilgrims when he spoke. However, for more in-depth discussions, Massasoit next sent Squanto, who was **fluent** in English from his time away. Squanto became the tribe's translator. The Pilgrims were stunned to hear someone speaking their own language so well. They agreed to make a deal of peace and friendship with Massasoit. The two groups also agreed to trade with each other. They promised to help each other if anyone

Squanto showed the Pilgrims how his people planted corn.

attacked them. Massasoit decided to let Squanto help the Pilgrims learn how to live on the land.

Before they met Squanto, half of the Pilgrims had died because they didn't have enough food. Squanto changed that. He showed the Pilgrims where to fish and hunt. He taught them how to grow the foods the Native Americans ate. Thanks to Squanto, the Pilgrims soon had lots of food.

Thanksgiving

To celebrate, the Pilgrims had a big feast. During the celebration, they shot their guns in the air. When the Native Americans heard the gunshots, they thought the Pilgrims were getting ready to fight. Massasoit then rushed to their **settlement** with 90 of his warriors.

When the Native Americans arrived, they saw that the Pilgrims were hunting for a feast. They decided to help. They killed five deer to add to the meal. This harvest celebration lasted three days. Today, many people think of this as the first Thanksgiving ever celebrated in America.

Squanto decided to live with the Pilgrims. He became a guide for leaders like William Bradford. He had a **devious** side too. It's believed that sometimes he told the Native Americans lies about the Pilgrims. It's also believed that he told the Pilgrims lies about the Native Americans. However, for the most part, he was a big help to the Pilgrims.

In 1622, Squanto guided a group of new Pilgrims to a Native American village near present-day Pleasant Bay, Massachusetts. At some point, he got sick and died. The Pilgrims lost a helper and friend.

The Pilgrims had a feast to celebrate learning how to hunt and farm.

Samoset (*right*) introduced Squanto to the Pilgrims.

DIFFERENT WORLDS

The 1600s was part of a time called the Age of Exploration. People in Europe were exploring Asia, Africa, and the Americas. The explorers found beavers and foxes in North America. Europeans liked the furs from these animals and used them to make hats and coats. For many years, Europeans came to North America to get furs. They later began to settle in North America for other reasons too. It's important to understand the lives of the settlers to better understand why Squanto's help was so important.

Settling America

Some Europeans decided to come to America to live permanently. They came for different reasons. Some thought it would be an adventure. Some hoped they could start a farm or a business. The Pilgrims couldn't worship the way they wanted in England, so they left for a new adventure in a new land that would let them worship however they pleased.

London in the 1600s was crowded and busy, and some parts were very dirty .

Colonists in Jamestown, Virginia, build a fort to protect themselves against attacks from Native Americans.

America was very different from Europe. In Europe, there were big cities. There were theaters, churches, and shops. In America, there were little villages. The houses were simple buildings. They were made of logs, tree bark, or animal skins. They belonged to the Native Americans.

The first permanent English settlement in America was at Jamestown in Virginia. The Native Americans and settlers traded with each other, but they didn't always get along. The settlers took food from the Native Americans. They built houses on their land. Before long, more settlers arrived. They cut down trees and killed many animals. They took more land. The unhappy Native Americans attacked the English communities, and the settlers attacked the Native Americans.

Fast Fact

Some Wampanoag men wore eagle feathers in their headbands. They earned the feathers by doing something brave.

THE GREAT CHIEF

"Massasoit" was a title, not a name. It meant "great sachem," or "great chief." Each Wampanoag tribe had its own leader, or sachem, but Massasoit was the main leader of all the Wampanoag tribes. His real name, Ousemequin, meant "Yellow Feather."

Massasoit was a wise leader. He traded with visitors from Europe, but he didn't go on their ships. He made friends with the Pilgrims. Squanto was his **go-between**. He carried and delivered messages between Massasoit and the Pilgrims. Peace between Massasoit's people and the Pilgrims lasted 50 years.

This statue of Massasoit stands near Plymouth Rock in Massachusetts.

Starting Out

The Pilgrims started out the same way as the Virginia settlers. They arrived in the winter, when it was too late to plant crops. They had to find food another way. They found where the Native Americans hid their corn, took it, and ate it to survive.

That first winter, many Pilgrims died. Of the 102 people who arrived in Massachusetts, only 53 were still living by the spring. Women suffered the worst loss in numbers.

The Pilgrims and the Wampanoag people eventually had a more peaceful relationship than the relationship between the Virginia settlers and the Native Americans they met. That was because of the deal Squanto helped make between the Pilgrims and Massasoit.

Massasoit protected the Pilgrims from Native Americans who wanted to fight. Squanto explained to the Pilgrims how to get along with the Native Americans. He helped them make peace deals with different tribes. Squanto also taught them how to grow corn and other important crops.

Without Squanto, the Pilgrims may have all died. They would have starved or been killed. Squanto lived with the Pilgrims for only about a year and a half. That was long enough for the Pilgrim community to learn enough from him to survive and grow stronger.

Wetus were different sizes depending on the season. In the summer, families lived near the ocean in a small wetu like this one. In colder weather, they moved inland and lived in a larger wetu.

Fast Fact

The Patuxet lived in homes called *wetus*. A wetu was a type of house built from poles that made a dome shape. It was covered in grasses or tree bark, depending on the season.

This carving of Squanto's head is one way he's been honored.

REMEMBERING SQUANTO

Squanto is remembered as a helper to foreigners in his land, a kind of early American **diplomat**, and an ambassador for Massasoit. Today, people can look to him as an example of how to treat others new to their communities or countries. His story reminds people that to help everyone succeed, people need to work together. Today, Squanto's legacy lives on, and the most famous part of his story is celebrated every November. He's a **role model** to all.

Squanto's Help

To the Wampanoag, Squanto was important because of his many talents and ideas. Along with Samoset, Squanto worked to make friends with the

Fast Fact

Harvard, the first American college, started a school in 1656 that was free for Native Americans. The first person to graduate was a Wampanoag.

Pilgrims. He showed them how to survive in difficult winters, how to grow crops, and how to work with Native Americans. The story of Squanto and his relationship with the Pilgrims shows that different groups of people can work together and learn from each other. Both the Native Americans

SQUANTO IN POP CULTURE

Squanto's story is in many history books and has been featured in popular culture. Biographies and articles have been written about his life and the impact he had on the communities in which he was involved. His story is also shown on television and in movies.

The Peanuts cartoon "Mayflower Voyagers" shows Squanto helping the Pilgrims. In addition, a movie was made about his life called *Squanto: A Warrior's Tale.* We don't know much about Squanto's life, so many scenes in *Squanto: A Warrior's Tale* are made up. The movie tells how some people think Squanto might have lived.

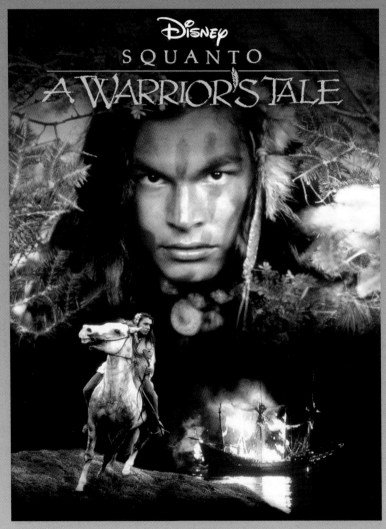

The 1994 movie *Squanto: A Warrior's Tale* tells Squanto's story from the time he was kidnapped to the first Thanksgiving.

and Pilgrims wanted to live, work, and survive. For a while, with Squanto's help, they did that side by side.

Pilgrim Ideas

Without Squanto, the Pilgrims may not have lived long and their ideas may have been lost forever. Many of these ideas helped shaped the future of what's now the United States. Ideas the Pilgrims developed in America included democracy, which is the form of government the United States uses today. In a democracy, citizens have a say in how the government runs and can vote for their leaders.

The Pilgrims met with Massasoit to make peace and work together.

In 17th-century England, the king made most of the decisions. The king chose **governors** to run colonies for him. The Virginia colony had a governor, and the Pilgrims were supposed to go to Virginia. However, after winds blew their ship away from Virginia and they landed in Massachusetts, they had to figure out what to do without a governor to lead them or make laws. The Pilgrims decided that people could rule themselves. The Mayflower Compact was the first example of English people ruling themselves in the New World.

If Squanto had not helped the Pilgrims survive, the history of democracy in the United States may have been very different!

In Squanto's Memory

Even though Squanto was a leader in his community, he is not honored today in the same way some more famous Native Americans of the past are. No statues or **monuments** exist to celebrate him. Some artists have imagined what he looked like, especially at the first Thanksgiving. However, his image isn't as well known as that of Massasoit, who has many **sculptures** around the United States. Very few details are actually known about Squanto's life, so his story isn't as well known as the stories of other Native American heroes. However, that doesn't mean he was less important than those heroes!

> ### Fast Fact
> Although there are no statues of Squanto in the United States, many go to Massasoit's statue near Plymouth Rock, Massachusetts, to remember him.

Squanto's life wasn't easy. He was kidnapped and sent far from his home. However, after he returned, he used skills he'd learned while away to help the people around him. He became an **interpreter** and helper to the Pilgrims in their time of need. He showed everyone around him—Native American or Pilgrim—that **barriers** could be broken and friendships could be made no matter where you came from. Above all, he helped the Pilgrims and Native Americans have peace for a time.

Other Native Americans, such as Massasoit, have been honored with statues. Squanto has not.

King Philip's War was one of the bloodiest in American history.

Remembering Squanto Today

Squanto may not have any cities, memorials, or buildings named after him, but he's still an important figure who is remembered today. In saving the Pilgrims, he saved their ideas and helped those ideas become part of American culture. Maybe the best way to remember Squanto is to tell the story of what we think of as the first Thanksgiving. Through this story—and other stories about Squanto's life—key ideas about cooperation were passed down from generation to generation and still exist in American society today.

On Thanksgiving, many families enjoy the same foods Squanto probably shared with his Pilgrim friends.

THINK ABOUT IT!

Use these questions to help you think more deeply about this topic.

1. Why do you think so few details are known about Squanto's life?

2. Why do you think Squanto helped the Pilgrims even after being kidnapped by white explorers?

3. What was a way Squanto gained the Pilgrims' trust? Why did it work?

4. How did Squanto help the Pilgrims' legacy survive?

5. What do you think is the most important part of Squanto's story?

TIMELINE

Squanto's Life	World Events
	1607 English colonists settle in Jamestown, Virginia.
1614 Squanto is kidnapped and goes to England.	
1616–1619 Diseases completely destroy Squanto's people and village.	
1619 Squanto returns to his village and finds it empty.	
	1620 The ship *Mayflower* brings Pilgrims to Plymouth, Massachusetts.
1621 Squanto and other Native Americans celebrate a feast with the Pilgrims.	
1622 Squanto becomes ill and dies.	

1675
King Philip's War, named after Massasoit's son, begins. It ends 50 years of peace between the Wampanoag and the Pilgrims.

GLOSSARY

barrier: Something that stops someone from doing something, such as a wall, a fence, or rules.

devious: Willing to lie or trick people to get what they want.

diplomat: A person who speaks to another country or a group of people in order to start a peaceful friendship or business partnership with them.

fluent: Knowing a language or subject completely.

go-between: A person who carries messages between two other people.

governor: A person who rules an area, such as a state or colony.

interpreter: A person who listens to a person speaking in one language and then explains in another language what the person said.

monument: An object, usually a building, that honors someone for their accomplishments in history.

puberty: The physical process of children becoming adults.

role model: A person who is a good example to others.

sculpture: A carved piece of stone or wood, usually showing a person, animal, or other object.

settlement: A beginning community in an area.

FIND OUT MORE

Books

Bruchac, Joseph. *Squanto's Journey: The Story of the First Thanksgiving*. New York, NY: Harcourt, 2007.

Holub, Joan. *What Was the First Thanksgiving?* New York, NY: Grosset & Dunlap, 2013.

McDonald, Julie. *The True Story of Squanto and the First Thanksgiving*. Amazon Digital Services, 2017.

Websites

Crash Course US History: When Is Thanksgiving?
www.youtube.com/watch?v=o69TvQqyGdg
This educational video explores the different colonies that began America, and includes the story of the arrival of the Pilgrims and Squanto's role in that story.

Ducksters: Squanto Biography
www.ducksters.com/history/colonial_america/pilgrims_plymouth_colony.php
This written story and video about the Pilgrims also tells about the Wampanoag and Squanto.

Plimoth Plantation
www.plimoth.org
This website explores the history of the *Mayflower* and the Plymouth settlement the Pilgrims created in 1620.

INDEX

A
ambassador, 23

B
barrier, 26

C
corn, 13–14, 20
crops, 20, 23

D
democracy, 25–26
devious, 15
diplomat, 23
diseases, 14

E
England, 8–9, 11–12, 17, 25

F
fluent, 14

G
go-between, 19
governor, 25

I
interpreter, 26

M
Massasoit, 7, 14–15, 19–20, 23, 25–27
Mayflower, 8, 24
Mayflower Compact, 8–9, 25
monuments, 26

P
Patuxet, 7, 11–12, 14, 21
Pilgrims, 6–11, 14–17, 19–20, 23–27
puberty, 20

R
role model, 23

S
Samoset, 6–7, 14, 16, 23
sculptures, 26
settlement, 15

T
Thanksgiving, 5, 11, 15, 26–27
tribe, 5, 7, 9, 11, 13–14, 19–20, 23

W
Wampanoag, 4, 7, 11–14, 18–20, 23, 27
wetu, 21